Making Mosaics

Making Mosaics

John Berry

Studio Vista London

Watson-Guptill Publications New York

General Editor Jean Richardson
© John Berry 1966
Published in London by Studio Vista Limited
Blue Star House, Highgate Hill, London N19
and in New York by Watson-Guptill Publications
165 West 46th Street, New York
Library of Congress Catalog Card Number 67-10437
Set in Folio Grotesque 8 and 9 pt.
Printed in the Netherlands
by N.V. Grafische Industrie Haarlem

Contents

Introduction

Mosaic is a durable, easily cleaned, colourful surface which, in the last few years, has been rediscovered as an attractive and useful material for exterior and interior decorations.

Mosaic making is traditionally a process of producing pictures or patterns by cementing together small pieces of stone, glass, etc., of various colours. The three main forms in which mosaic is used today are on walls and wall panels, paths and paved areas in the garden, and for counter, bar and coffee table tops.

Almost any material that is permanent and reasonably light in weight can be made into a mosaic. Apart from the word 'mosaic', the word most frequently used in this book is 'tesserae', which comes originally from the Greek via a Latin derivation meaning 'four cornered'. I shall use the word to describe the pieces of any material that together make up the surface of a mosaic. These small tesserae have an almost infinite colour range and reflective quality.

My aim has been to include all relevant information about the making and designing of mosaics that will guide and help both the beginner and the more advanced mosaicist. In the following pages you will find out about materials, tools (and where to obtain them), how to stick and support your mosaics and also how to start designing and drawing for them. I have included a chapter describing a number of mosaic projects to make for yourself, and these projects will give you some idea of the varied scope and application of modern mosaics. You will find one chapter devoted to making your own ceramic mosaic materials, and if you have already had some experience with ceramics, this chapter should suggest new possibilities to you.

I believe that it is essential for our development as human beings that we should reject a passive role with our recreations and hobbies. I hope, therefore, that this book may help towards stimulating and encouraging you to explore the wonderful world of your own creative potential.

1 Types of mosaic materials

I believe it is true to say that almost anything that has a solid shape and can be stuck to a rigid surface may be used as a mosaic material.

Such total freedom can, of course, end in total confusion, both for the mosaicist and for the finished design. I intend in this chapter to make a list of some of the vast variety of substances suitable for use in the designing and assembly of mosaics. I shall start with the traditional Italian glass smalti, but I do not wish to give the impression that this is necessarily a list in any sort of order of preference. The art of mosaic encourages the imagination in many ways, not least in the adaptation and application of all sorts of un-orthodox materials.

Mosaic tesserae may be either porous or non-porous, and this is an important point to remember in any pre-planning of a mosaic project. For instance, porous tesserae used outside the house in an exposed position are liable to be cracked by frost. The porosity of tesserae in turn determines the suitable adhesive, cement or backing to use with them.

1 Byzantine smalti

Glass tile measuring about $\frac{3}{8}'' \times \frac{1}{2}''$ (Fig. 5). Made in large sheets then split along its face side, this brittle uneven surface gives the magnificent light and colour reflections found in the mosaics of Ravenna and Constantinople (Istanbul). Byzantine smalti have probably the largest colour range available and are also the most expensive of manufactured mosaic materials. The glass used is coloured by the addition of metallic oxides. For example, the addition of cobalt oxide makes a rich ultramarine blue, copper oxide makes green, lead and iron oxides make the yellow range. The more subtle colours are derived from mixtures of more than one oxide. Tin oxide is used to make a colour opaque. With gold and silver tesserae, a thin metal sheet is applied to the front of a piece of clear glass and then sandwiched beneath a fused glass film above. For a richer gold effect, the bottom piece of glass is usually red in colour. Because of surface irregularity, Byzantine smalti are not suitable for use where a flat surface is essential (i.e. table tops etc.).

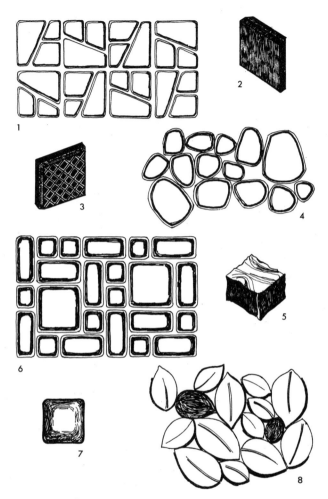

2 Vitreous glass tesserae

The standard sizes are $\frac{3}{4}'' \times \frac{3}{4}''$ and $\frac{3}{8}'' \times \frac{3}{8}''$ (Fig. 2). The glass is melted by heat and poured into moulds. This process forms a bevel or chamfer on the sides and a pattern of square ridges underneath (Fig. 3). The ridges help in forming a firmer grip for the adhesive.

Some glass tesserae exported from Italy are pasted face down on one foot square sheets of paper (for ease of assembly in the indirect method, see chapter 4). If you wish to remove the paper from the tesserae, soak the sheet in warm water and peel off. Suppliers of mosaic in small quantities or in kit form may sell the tesserae loose in bags according to colour. Reds, oranges, yellows and golds are the most expensive. Vitreous glass tesserae do not deteriorate with age, and if firmly supported they are almost indestructable. They are impervious to staining, easy to clean and do not hold the dirt. Moulded glass mosaic has a smooth surface, therefore it is most suitable for all types of table or counter tops.

3 Vitrified ceramic mosaic

Made from non-porous fired clay, available in glazed and unglazed surfaces (Fig. 7). There are various sizes; the most common range from $\frac{3}{4}'' \times \frac{3}{4}''$ to $1'' \times 1''$. It is supplied in paper faced sheets $12'' \times 12''$. Ceramic mosaic is the cheapest of the manufactured mosaic materials and is made in most countries that have a ceramic industry. There is a wide colour range, mostly pastel and muted colours. Gold and silver are also available. There are many surface textures from glossy flecked to matt speckled. The tesserae are supplied in a wide variety of shapes including unglazed block random (Fig. 6), hexagonal mixtures, glazed trapezium (Fig. 1), cushion edge glazed squares, glazed block random and glazed pebble and leaf mixtures (Figs 4 and 8). With such a comprehensive range of shapes it is not usual to cut them any further by hand. This does not of course apply to the standard $4'' \times 4''$ or $6'' \times 6''$ ceramic wall or floor tiles. The tesserae are usually supplied in one foot square pasted sheets. Random patterns interlock, resulting in almost invisible joints. The fixing of ceramic tesserae can be carried out with proprietary tile adhesives and grouted (see chapter 6), or by traditional methods with sand and cement. Ceramic mosaic is an ideal material for the beginner. It can be mixed with small quantities of the more expensive glass smalti to produce brilliant colour contrasts to its more subdued colours.

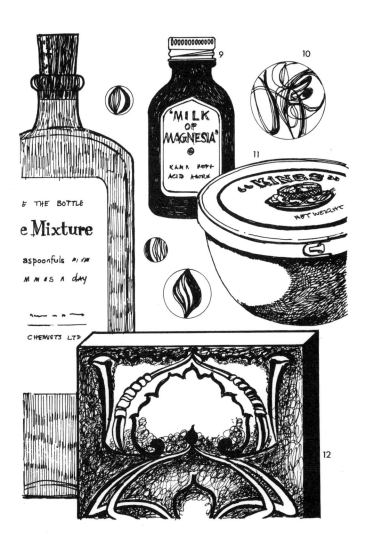

E THE BOTTLE

e Mixture

aspoonfuls ᴀɪ ɪᴍ

ᴍ ᴍ ᴀs ᴀ day

CHEMISTS LTD

9

'MILK OF MAGNESIA'

ᴋᴀᴍᴀ ᴍᴏᴘᴛ
ᴀᴄɪᴅ ᴀᴍᴏʀᴇ

10

11

"KINGS"

NET WEIGHT

12

4 Ceramic floor and wall tiles

The standard size is 4" x 4" or 6" x 6". Floor tiles are usually limited in colour to red and blue-blacks, and although they are very strong they are also very thick. Try if you can to obtain some Victorian transfer-printed decorated floor tiles (Fig. 12) from building demolition sites. Another source for decorative Victorian tiles is back yards of junk shops. Here, rotting out in the open, you may find old wash stands with a splash back set in tiles. There may be a firm making tiled fireplace surrounds near where you live; if so, you may find that you can collect broken or chipped tiles for next to nothing. Ceramic tiles usually need shattering into smaller pieces with a hammer or hard piece of timber. Remember always to break tiles beneath a thick cloth or sack to prevent broken chips flying about. For more accurate cutting, use either mosaic cutters or a standard glass cutter. Apart from their obvious availability and cheapness, sizeable pieces of broken tile are very useful in covering large areas of background in your mosaic designs.

5 Coloured glass

There are two other sources of coloured glass apart from the traditional smalti. Small off-cuts of coloured glass can be obtained from shops specialising in glass (window or mirror) cutting. The colour range may not be very great, but usually the same shop can put you in touch with a supplier of genuine stained glass. Once again, the deeper and richer colours of stained glass are also more expensive.

A much more economical way of obtaining coloured glass is from glass bottles and containers such as beer, wine and liqueur bottles, medicine bottles of all kinds, not forgetting the wonderful blue in milk of magnesia (Fig. 9) and eye lotion bottles. Some fishpaste (Fig. 11), cheese and haircream is still packed in a variety of white opaque glass jars. Bottle glass is thick, chunky and cheap. It can also be razor sharp, so you must take the maximum precaution when breaking bottle glass by wearing an eye shield, thick gloves and an apron, and make sure the glass bottles etc. are thoroughly covered by a thick layer of sacking before you start hammering.

6 Marbles

Large and small glass marbles (Fig 10) with their lovely embedded spiral designs have all sorts of possible applications in mosaic. Try to cut or chip them to form approximate half spheres or domes, and don't forget to use a transparent adhesive. To exploit the luminosity inherent in glass marbles further, brush the chipped underneath part with aluminium paint before setting into your design.

7 Stone

Large stones of flint or granite make an excellent hardwearing material for garden or patio mosaics. In addition to these stones, there is a wide range in the size and colour of gravel. Builders merchants, gardening shops and fish and aquarium suppliers between them cover most available gravels and sands. Always make sure that the stones have been sieved and washed. If they have not, you should sieve and wash them yourself at least three times, then dry the stones thoroughly before using. Cut and dressed stone such as marble and Portland stone may be obtained as off-cuts (also sometimes as chippings) from monumental masons. Slate is another very lovely natural stone that can be used outside or inside for mosaic panels. Old billiard table tops, Victorian wash stands and broken roof slates will provide the cheapest slate. I have found that the Eclipse No. 66 General Purpose saw is very efficient in cutting marble, Portland stone and slate. You can also use a hacksaw, but remember that all these stones are comparatively soft, so make sure you don't force or twist the blade during sawing.

8 Wood

Wood strips or laths of the rarer coloured and figured woods like teak, mahogany and rosewood may be used to produce rich warm textures in your mosaics. The wood strips usually look most effective fixed down on their thinner edge. This allows you to produce long directional curves impossible with other materials. Fine quality woods need only be polished with number 0 grade steel wool dipped in a little pure linseed oil. Don't forget to rub along with the wood grain and not across it. Soft wood strips or blocks are lighter but not so flexible; they require sealing

13

with at least two coats of poly-urethane clear varnish. Man-made wood and in particular $\frac{1}{4}''$ thick, oil tempered hardboard can be used in almost all types of weather conditions. If you want to fix the hardboard on its edge, remove the textured side with sandpaper. The hardboard can be polished with a silicone wax polish that will produce a deep dark sheen. You can also paint wood any colour, but I would advise against this for the beginner, until you know exactly what sort of effect you are after.

9 Metal

Any metal that is light and does not tarnish is suitable. First in this category are the large variety of galvanised nails with all sorts of flat and domed heads (Fig. 17). One great advantage of using nails is that they can be stuck into the support panel without the need for any adhesive. Next, I would suggest experimenting with all diameter sizes of aluminium alloy tubes. Cut the tubes (with a hacksaw) into collections of different lengths before arranging them into your design. Cut aluminium L, T, U shaped sections (bars) in the same way. For inside mosaic wall panels, the limited use of aluminium cooking foil can be very attractive as a light reflective, non tarnishing, lightweight material. Always use a contact or epoxy resin adhesive for attaching metals to your supports.

10 Other people's rubbish

Don't let your friends throw away smashed earthenware or china bowls, cups etc. (Fig. 13). They should be broken into small pieces and kept in colour graded cardboard shoe boxes, and you will always have a versatile stock of ceramic mosaic. A list of suitable mosaic materials salvaged from the dustbin is almost endless, here are some of them: - broken mirror glass; bone and plastic buttons (Fig. 16); cheap jewellery (Fig. 14) - extract the stones and discard the setting; door knobs and finger plates; bottle corks; Formica and Perspex (Plexiglas) fittings and so on.

If you live near the sea or perhaps when you are on holiday, make a collection of shells, particularly the iridescent mother of pearl saddle oyster's shell (Fig. 15). Sea smoothed and rounded, red, grey and black building bricks are also useful in creating new colours and textures. In particular I would recommend small strips of driftwood, scoured and bleached by the sea and sun. These thin pieces of broken plank have a grey silvery sheen that is quite unique. After thoroughly soaking and washing all material recovered from the beach (to remove salt), dry and attach to your support panel with tile adhesive or contact glue.

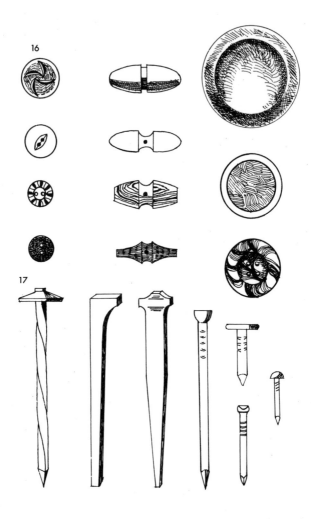

2 Design and drawing materials

Probably the most misunderstood chapter in art and craft books is the chapter on design. There are several reasons for this, but the main one is that a comprehensive explanation of only one aspect of making a design needs a complete and lavishly illustrated book to itself. Such books in any case are rare, but I have attempted to list a few in the section for further reading.

Within the limits of this chapter I propose to make a series of general statements on design to guide you as your ambitions develop. Before going any further, I want to make it quite clear that I do not believe that there are people who are 'just no good at art' etc., etc. The fact that you have either bought or borrowed this book proves that you have a real interest (however timid or latent that interest may be) in making and creating something of your own.

I hold no prejudice against any method that gets the beginner started. If you are certain that a ready-made mosaic kit (that includes just the right amount of tools and materials plus a design for you to copy) will give you confidence, then make a start with mosaics this way.

Sooner or later, if your interest in mosaic persists, you will want to discard the ready-made kit because you will have to admit that anyone with patience and reasonably good eyesight can easily make the same mosaic from an identical kit.

I am sure the worst problem when setting out to create a design from 'nothing' is how to choose and come to a decision on what to design. Perhaps we should remember that we confidently exercise our capacities to select and decide when the choice is a car, clothes or a holiday. In our choice of car or clothes we are usually very capable people who know what we want. We are able to arrive at our final decision by considering such requirements as available time, size, finance etc., in conjunction with our accumulated experience and personal intuition. Of course all these considerations have to relate (in varying proportions) to each other before we make our final decision and choice. Therefore I cannot understand why we should not apply the same method to a similar choice and selection problem as designers. For example, if you want to design a mosaic topped coffee table, you will probably have to consider the problems of your available time, size required and finance, assisted and influenced by your experience and intuition.

Perhaps I should elaborate a little on a design-choice-method that includes 'experience and intuition' as part of the formula. Your memorised experience may be made up of knowledge remembered from your past mistakes. Intuition (direct or immediate insight) could be described as a short cut system to a design solution; in other words, you make a choice or decision based on a personal 'hunch'.

You will find that a commonsense approach to design that is an amalgamation of your functional (useful) and your intuitive (emotional) requirements will be easily recognised and appreciated as your own individual work.

One last general point, a basic approach to design should be flexible enough to be applied to any medium or material including mosaic.

Nobody can give you the exact answer or recipe for a design. What I can attempt to do is to make a short list of suggestions that may save you making unnecessary and disappointing mistakes.

1 Simplicity

I cannot over-emphasise for the beginner the importance of simple, straightforward designs which will require a minimum of intricate cutting and placing of the tesserae. You will also start to develop your own design experience by a rational, step-by-step method at your own pace.

2 Shape (area)

At first you will probably use pieces of mosaic that are roughly square or rectangular. The shape of these units suggests that your first designs could be based on simple geometric shapes like the square, circle and triangle. These shapes can be varied to produce rectangles, parallelograms, ellipses, diamonds. If you get tired of designing only geometric patterns, you could place, for example, different flower shapes into a pattern of circles and ellipses. Try fitting architecture (houses, shops, churches, stations, garages) into a basic geometric arrangement of squares and triangles.

3 Colour

Limit your mosaic colour schemes at first to one colour by using all the shades of one of your favourite colours plus the addition of black and white. The black may be used as the drawing line around shapes, and the white can be used to emphasise the vivid, saturated colours by acting as an area of contrast, for instance, in the background.

Try to develop your colour appreciation in different ways. Think of colour as affecting the spectator like music, and put your colours together in harmonious compositions. Don't think in terms of literal or 'local' colour (e.g., the sky is blue, sun yellow, grass green, the house red etc.). Think of the basic colour sensations of blueness, yellowness, greeness and redness, and use your colours to create these sensations.

4 Design

It is important to understand the particular possibilities and limitations of your mosaic material. Don't try to make a mosaic look like an oil painting or photograph. It just can't be done, and even if you try the result will look awkward and visually irritating. Do remember that you are using hard, multi-coloured units that are very permanent, moisture and heat-resistant, easily cleaned, and in some cases may be used in relief (tesserae can 'stick out' from their background area). If you consider the varied qualities contained in mosaic material plus the method of assembly, you should start to design with both the limitations and possibilities of mosaic clearly in your mind. You should start to 'think' in mosaic terms before and during the designing and making of a mosaic.

5 Scale

A variety in size of the tesserae is visually less monotonous. Usually large areas of the background will need larger size pieces than the smaller, more detailed parts of your design.

6 Textures

Take or collect photographs, postcards and slides of all the textures you find around you at home or on holiday. Use

19

the camera lens in close up to photograph such things as brickwork, wooden fencing, carpets, rocks and pebbles, stacked timber, displays of tins and packets in grocery super-markets etc. Aerial photographs of cities, ruins and landscape often suggest pattern-like textures.

7 Scrapbooks

The best way to collect and file all the design information that interests and stimulates you from the vast variety of coloured magazines, brochures and photographs you may collect, is to prepare your own design scrapbook. This scrapbook will bring together all your personally selected visual information and may be constantly added to.

8 Paper mosaic

After the preliminary sketching stage when you are designing a mosaic, it is sometimes a good idea to make either a half or even a full size colour 'rough' out of paper mosaic. To do this, take a large variety of coloured paper (plus white paper you have coloured) and cut it into squares and rectangles equivalent in size and proportion to your mosaic materials. You can then move these paper 'tesserae' about, exchange them, try one against another, brilliant against dull and so on. Use a paste or rubber solution to stick them down on to a sheet of paper. With paper mosaic you will be able to vary your design ideas before committing yourself to the final permanent material.

Finally, a few remarks about enlarging procedure and drawing materials.

One of the most common problems once you have worked out a satisfactory design sketch is to enlarge it to exactly the finished mosaic size. All you have to do is to draw, for example, $\frac{1}{2}''$ squares in a grid over your original sketch. You can draw the grid on tracing paper if you don't want to mark the original. If you wish to double the size, take a sheet of paper twice the size of the sketch and draw $1''$ squares all over it, also in a grid. You can now copy exactly the original drawings from square to square. Coloured areas may be enlarged in the same way. You can increase to any reasonable proportion by multiplying the size of the original grid. The same principle can be used for a decrease in size as well. Remember that if you are enlarging for the indirect method of laying mosaic, the enlarged sketch must be on tracing paper so that the drawing can be reversed.

Drawing materials

At first your drawing and designing materials need only consist of several sheets of brown paper (or newspaper) and some black, white and coloured chalks. Pin or tape the paper to a flat rigid surface such as a table, wall or floor. You are now ready to make a start at producing your own mosaic designs and cartoons.

1 Tracing paper is necessary when you want to reverse your design for the indirect method of making a mosaic. Tracing paper is also useful when you want to change only a small part of a design. You can trace both the alteration and the rest of the design from the original drawing quickly and accurately.

2 Carbon paper can be used to copy or repeat an original design on to another surface.

3 Graph paper (Fig. 18) can be bought in varying size squares from about 1/16 " upwards. The squares approximate roughly to the proportions of glass and ceramic tesserae. When a design is made on graph paper, you have a quick handy reference of the quantity, type, colour and sizes that will be required for the finished mosaic.

4 Half or Imperial size drawing board. An alternative is a new, flush-sided door made from hardboard upon a softwood frame 6' x 2'6" (check that all corners are square). This is the cheapest, largest and not too heavy support for full size designs and cartoons.

5 Drawing compass. A simple, robust, school quality compass for drawing curves and circles, or the large radius compass screwed on to a steel ruler (Figs 21 and 22).

6 Clear plastic 45° and 60° set squares (Fig. 19).

7 T squares. You could make your own, suitable for the 'door' type of drawing board, out of ¼" hardboard for the blade and 3" x 1" beech for the T.

8 Soft, plastic, flexible curve for repeating multiple complex curves (Fig. 20).

9 Steel rule (included in your workshop requirements).

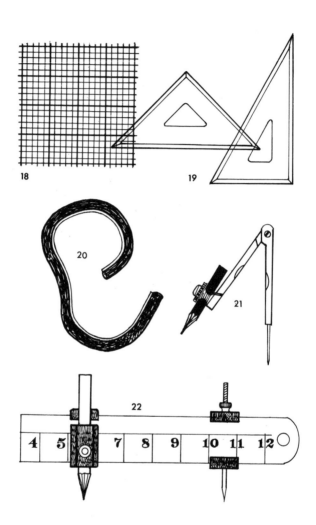

18

19

20

21

22

4 5 7 8 9 10 11 12

10 Pencils. A selection of B and H grades.

11 Charcoal. Buy the largest and thickest sticks for sketching in your outline ideas.

12 Square section oil crayons in stick form (all colours). Square section conté crayons (black, red and white). Felt pens with flat tipped points. All these drawing materials suggest the shape of pieces of tesserae and will contribute to your ability to 'think' and design in mosaic equivalents.

13 The softest and largest rubber available. The so-called 'kneaded' rubber is another good variety.

14 Water soluble paint. School quality powder colour mixed with water is cheap and reliable. For a full range of bright colours, use the more expensive Winsor & Newton's designers' colours or any poster colours. For more permanent colours, use Pelikan 'Plaka' range or Rowney's 'Cryla' colours.

15 Brushes. Square tipped, hard hog bristle are suitable. The softer Chinese 'wolf' and 'goat' hair brushes are also very good. A number of $\frac{1}{2}''$ and 1'' household decorators brushes will be needed for large, full scale cartoons.

16 Assorted sheets of coloured paper (construction paper), gummed if possible, for making preliminary paper mosaics.

17 Roll of 1'' wide Scotch tape and 2'' wide gummed paper strip. These tapes can be used for sticking paper down on to drawing boards, as the tape does not mark the surface of the board. You can also use tape to stick several pieces of paper together to make one large sheet for your wall or garden mosaic designs.

18 Reducing glass. As its name implies, when you look at your design through a reducing glass the design appears smaller and more compact. What the reduced image also shows, much more clearly, is the parts of your design that are out of balance and proportion in area, colour and texture.

19 Pantograph for enlarging original designs. This does not normally enlarge to a very large scale, but it does enlarge very accurately. It is usually made of wood with multiple adjustable slots, and as you trace over your original drawing with one end of the pantograph, it simultaneously makes a larger version on another sheet of paper.

3 Getting started

In the chapters so far, I have described most of the technical and practical background that has to be understood before you can actually start making mosaics.

Before going on to the projects to make, I would strongly recommend three simple but important exercises on texture and colour, reflected light, and placing and setting.

So often readers of craft handbooks follow all the practical instructions and buy all (often more than required) of the materials and tools, only to be disappointed with their first results because the design is both weak and dull. Their genuine interest in a subject only survives, if at all, by copying other artists' work, which is not very satisfying.

I do not intend to offer a short cut to good design, but I do believe that if these three exercises are followed carefully and repeated if necessary, then some understanding of the problems found in designing a mosaic should have been achieved.

Texture and colour

Texture, that is, the surface quality in mosaic, can vary as much as the colour. In order to appreciate this in a practical way, make the following texture and colour sample.

1 Unless you wish your texture and colour sample to be a permanent reference chart in your workshop, I suggest you place the tesserae in a bed of plasticine rolled out to about $\frac{3}{4}''$ thick (Fig. 24). You can buy white or coloured plasticine by the pound from any of the larger artists' materials shops. Using plasticine allows you to experiment in a variety of arrangements; at the same time, you can leave the work over long periods of time without it becoming permanent.

2 Divide your pancake of plasticine into several simple geometric sections by lightly inscribing lines with the tip of a pencil (Fig. 23).

3 Start with a primary colour, let us say blue, and assemble in their separate containers all the pieces of blue material suitable for a mosaic that you can find.

For example, Italian glass mosaic, glazed and unglazed ceramic tile fragments, bottle glass, pebbles, stone (slate and marble), pieces of blue jewellery etc.

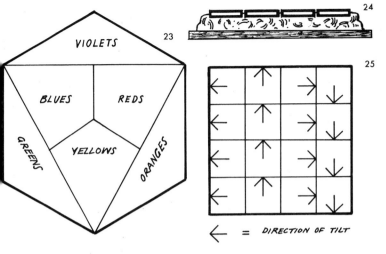

23
24
25

← = DIRECTION OF TILT

4 Now arrange all the blue bottle glass fragments in one part of the blue area, then all the bluish slate, and so on until the blue section is complete.

5 Fill in the other parts of the texture sample in the same way.

6 As an additional exercise (or you can incorporate it in the first arrangement), try placing some of the pieces on their sides at varying depths in the plasticine.

When the texture and colour sample is finished, it should be clear that the so called blues vary enormously according to the qualities of the materials. The size and the depth the pieces project from the background also develops this colour and texture variation.

A glossy surface gives quite a different visual effect from a piece with a matt surface, and a mottled or striated surface varies from a smooth plain one.

Look at the blue bottle glass and compare it with the slate area. Then look again and compare all the other areas.

Reflected light

I have already mentioned in the introduction that one of the inherent qualities of mosaic is the capacity of each individual piece to reflect light and colour in different directions depending on the surface angle of the tesserae.

These sparkling reflections give a suggestion of blurred movement not to be found in any other static medium.

1 Once again, roll out a pancake of plasticine about one foot square and place tesserae in rows from left to right.

2 Press with the unsharpened end of a pencil the left side edge of the first column of tesserae.

3 Next press the top edge of the next column and go on until you have completed four columns of tesserae, each column with a different edge tipped down.

4 With any remaining columns vary the exercise by tipping the same side in rows or areas of tesserae (Fig. 25).

5 Lift your board supporting the mosaic upright and take it over to a single light source, for example, a reading lamp in an otherwise dark room, or draw the curtains until only one small area of light is left to fall on the mosaic.

6 You can now see the infinite variety of reflected light and colour that is produced by the angle of setting.

In practice you will only be able to use this angled setting in upright wall type panels and not, for instance, in a coffee table requiring a reasonably flat surface.

Placing and setting the tesserae

It should be obvious by now that a single piece of tessera is a chunky rather awkward shape to handle.

In making a mosaic picture it does not matter if you want to create a design recording the things you see around you, or a so-called 'abstract' design or pattern that bears no relation to your surroundings.

The problem of placing and setting the small, hard blocks is the same. Therefore I would suggest that one of the best ways of analysing the flow and direction in the placing of tesserae is as follows:

1 Collect a series of coloured postcards, photographs and magazine illustrations covering all periods of mosaic art. Make sure that the picture is enlarged enough to show individual tesserae. So-called 'details' of a larger work usually show up clearly the placing of all pieces.

2 Take a piece of tracing paper (greaseproof cooking paper is not so good, but it will do). Then, with a pencil or pen, trace the outline tesserae of the design. When you have finished, go on and fill in the inside area (Fig. 26).

3 After a reasonably varied and comprehensive series of

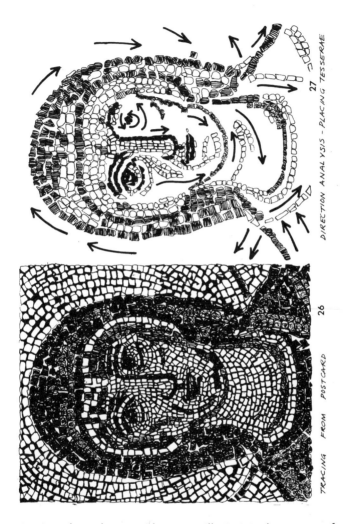

DIRECTION ANALYSIS – PLACING TESSERAE

27

TRACING FROM POSTCARD

26

tracings have been made, you will start to be aware of how the placing of the tesserae follows a flow and direction that suggests the contour of the form. For example, look at your tracings of such things as eyes, cheeks, folds in clothing (Fig. 27).

27

4 The direct and indirect methods

Direct method

With the direct method, each piece of mosaic tessera is set directly, by hand, into the mosaic adhesive. Tile cement or a contact glue are the most suitable adhesives for the beginner. As you lay each piece of mosaic into the glue bed, do not forget to leave the same width narrow gap between tesserae to allow for the final grouting. Strips of thick, flexible cardboard slipped in between the rows will help you to do this. You should remove the cardboard immediately after arranging two or three rows of mosaic, otherwise the card may stick to the adhesive.

Sometimes it is a good idea to make a full size design (cartoon) to guide you when you are using the direct method. The easiest way to do this is to draw a grid of squares (roughly the same size squares as the pieces of mosaic) all over your support panel.

1 Now paint your design in full colour, using household oil bound paints (Fig. 28).
2 When the paint is dry, apply a thin layer of clear adhesive. Use clear glue so that you will be able to see through to your design (Fig. 29).
3 Next set pieces of suitably shaped and coloured tesserae over the painted areas (Fig. 30).
4 If you use pieces of clear or translucent glass tesserae and stick them down over your brightly painted design, you should achieve an even greater variety of attractive coloured effects.

The direct method is also used for garden pebble and stone mosaics, and whenever the material making up the mosaic is embedded sideways on its shorter edge (Fig. 31). You should always use the direct method when parts of the mosaic project up from the surface in relief (Fig. 32).

The most important reason for using the direct method is to exploit fully the range of visual possibilities of the mosaic. By varying the angle and pitch of the face side of the tesserae (see chapter 3), you are able to control the reflected angle of light on the colours and surface textures of your mosaic. These sparkling reflections change, giving countless different combinations of colour and form as the observer moves in front of the mosaic.

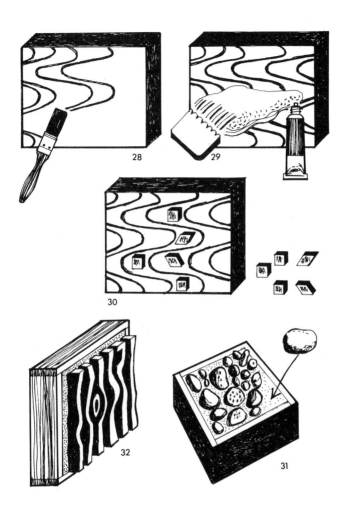

28

29

30

32

31

Indirect method

For large vertical surfaces the indirect method, applied in small areas at a time, is the most efficient way, because with other techniques the individual tesserae have a tendency to slip down.

The indirect (or reverse) method appears at first more complicated and difficult than the direct method. This need not be so; you should find no difficulty in achieving satisfactory results first time if you follow the procedure slowly and with care.

1 Measure and cut a piece of tracing or greaseproof paper slightly larger (1″ all round) than the outside dimensions of your mosaic panel (Fig. 33).

2 Draw a grid of squares slightly larger than the mosaic pieces you will use. This allows for grouting in between the tesserae (Fig. 34).

3 Now draw your design full size on to the tracing paper (Fig. 35).

4 Turn the tracing paper over and lay it down flat on some brown wrapping paper (Fig. 36).

5 Trace (using typewriter carbon paper) the now reversed design on to the brown paper (Fig. 37).

6 Paint the reversed design in full colour using water soluble paints, e.g. poster or designers' colour (Fig. 38).

7 Next turn your selected pieces of mosaic material over and stick them face down on the squared design with any paste or gum that will dissolve in water (Fig. 39).

8 Make sure you have placed the tesserae in the exact position (reversed) that you will want them to be in the finished mosaic.

9 Leave the paper and the mosaic pieces to dry.

10 Apply tile cement to wall or panel support. Spread the adhesive evenly, a small area at a time, with a notched spreader.

11 You can also thinly 'butter' the backs of the tesserae (that are pasted face down on the brown paper) with cement. This is done to even out the mosaic surface so that the sunken tiles or tesserae can reach the bed of cement on the wall or panel.

12 Pick up the sheet of papered mosaic with the mosaic outwards, away from you, and lower face side down into one corner of your mosaic support (Fig. 40).

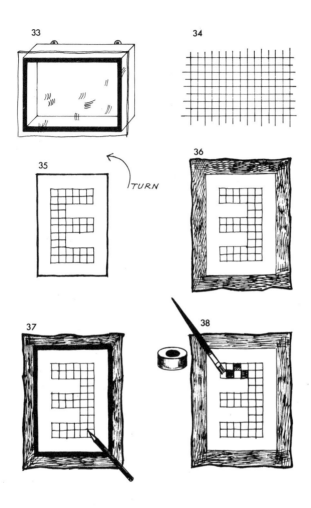

33

34

35

TURN

36

37

38

13 Press the back of the brown paper hard enough to force the cement into the spaces between the tesserae. Use a wooden rolling pin or broom handle, working from one corner of the mosaic to ensure even pressure all over (Fig. 41).

14 If any pieces of tesserae have sunk below the correct level, ease them out with an old screwdriver and add some cement to level them up.

15 After the mosaic has set firmly in its bed of permanent adhesive, moisten the brown paper two or three times with a sponge until the paper is thoroughly wet.

16 Screpe off paper with a plastic squeegee, finish cleaning with a copper or nylon scouring pad and warm water.

17 Leave the completed mosaic to stand for as long as possible (three to four days) before use.

It is possible to combine both the direct and indirect methods. The main advantage to the mosaicist is that it enables you to see and make alterations to your mosaic design the right way up, before applying it finally to a vertical surface.

This combined technique does of course take a little longer to assemble.

1 Draw your design full size and in full colour on strong paper. Make your design the way round you want it to appear in the finished mosaic (i.e., not reversed this time).

2 Now arrange your mosaic pieces on the paper, face side towards you. Alter and exchange the pieces until you are quite satisfied with your arrangement.

3 With a water solvent gum, paste the backs of the tesserae down on to the design paper. Allow it to thoroughly dry.

4 With the same paste stick a sheet of strong paper down on to the face side of the tesserae. You should now have a 'sandwich' of paper, tesserae and paper.

5 Place two drawing boards or two sheets of hardboard on either side of this sandwich and turn carefully over, so that the paper with the design is now on top.

6 Wet the top layer of paper (on the backs of the tesserae) and peel off carefully.

7 You have now arrived at stage 9 in the indirect method; proceed from here in exactly the same way.

If you are attaching a large area of mosaic, as soon as the tesserae are fixed down on the paper, cut the paper into smaller segments.

It is a good idea to cut irregularly shaped segments if possible. This is to stop a regular tile or brick like pattern formed by the joints appearing in your finished mosaic. In any case, only small manageable areas of adhesive should be spread for each application of a mosaic 'sheet'.

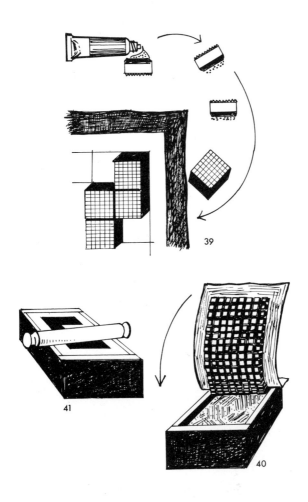

39

41

40

5 Backing and supports

When discussing the various types of mosaic supports, three major considerations have to be taken into account.

1 The foundation or panel supporting a mosaic must be solid and rigid, because vibration of any kind can soon crack a mosaic.

2 A support should be waterproof as it may be situated outside or in the high humidity of a kitchen or bathroom.

3 As well as being both solid and waterproof, a mosaic support must also be reasonably light in weight.

This does not only mean that it can be moved about without difficulty (coffee table, lamp), but that it will not pull its supporting wall down either (house nameplate, mosaic wall panel). Any baseboard over approximately 3' x 5' should be divided into several sections, otherwise the completed mosaic will be too heavy to lift and move about. For the smaller designs such as table mats, house nameplates, $\frac{1}{4}''$ thick oil tempered hardboard may be used. The textured side of the hardboard should receive the mosaic adhesive, and the texture will give a good 'key' to hold the glue to the base support.

Marine quality plywood from $\frac{1}{2}''$ to $\frac{3}{4}''$ thick can be used for large panels and coffee tables.

Blockboard, possibly a little cheaper, may be suitable, but it is not as strong as plywood.

All these supports, even the waterproof ones, should be brushed both sides and in particular on all edges with two coats of clear polyurethane varnish to make them completely waterproof. Don't forget that if you are preparing a wood support for wall hanging, you should screw heavy duty mirror brackets (Fig. 42) to the back of the base board before you lay your mosaic. Otherwise, you can easily cause a crack by screwing from the back into the finished tesserae.

The frames for your wall hangings may be either wood, metal or plastic. Soft plastic edging similar to the edge moulding used in kitchen cabinets is best for curved or round base boards.

The non-ferrous metals like aluminium, brass and copper make very attractive framing. They can be glued or screwed into position. Brass and copper can be lacquered with a clear varnish to prevent oxidisation.

Coloured ceramic tile mosaic by Simon Clark, aged 8

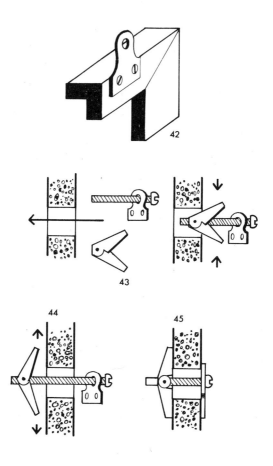

42

43

44

45

If you use wood mouldings for your frames, it is worth buying a mitre box to cut 45° corners accurately. The corners can then be glued and pinned with small panel pins. Drive the pins below the surface of the wood and fill the hole with plastic wood filler. You can make a temporary frame for your mosaic for the sticking down and grouting process. Then assemble your permanent frame after the dirty jobs have been completed.

There are many ready-made supports for small mosaics. For instance, a shallow aluminium pie tin has a lipped edge that forms its own 'frame'. Trays of all kinds with a shallow edge can be used as supports for your mosaics. An old coffee table that has been badly scratched or scorched makes an ideal ready-made support for a mosaic.

When fixing your smaller wall mosaics on to cavity walls made of lath and plaster, use spring toggle bolts. These bolts come in a variety of diameters and lengths and are galvanised against rusting.

1 Drill the hole. Unscrew toggle wings, push toggle screw through mirror bracket, screw toggle back on bolt. Press the two halves of the toggle together and push through hole (Fig. 43).

2 When the toggle is free of the hole on the inside of the cavity, it opens automatically by a spring (Fig. 44).

3 Pull toggle tight against the inside of the wall and tighten screw (Fig. 45).

To fix mosaic panels to concrete or brick, you can use expansion bolts (Fig. 96). These bolts have a shank that expands and tightens as it is screwed into place.

Heavy steel screws or bolts are suitable for attaching a panel to wood beams or partition studding, but make sure that the wood is at least 2" thick.

The traditional, all-in-one support and adhesive for mosaics is of course concrete. This concrete support is usually a sandwich of a coarse foundation layer with a finer top layer of cement to set the mosaic pieces into.

Most large scale architectural mosaics are set in concrete, and the same methods can be used in the garden or patio.

Small, concrete, mosaic slabs for the garden may be prefabricated in your workshop. Make simple wooden shuttering about 2' x 2' x 4" deep by using 1" x 4" sawn timber. You can make three corners of the shuttering planks hinged, with a hook and eye catch fastening the fourth corner (Fig. 47). Alternatively, you can attach right angle metal brackets that project 1" out from one corner of the four shuttering planks (Fig. 46). With the last method you can vary the size and proportion of your slabs.

The inside of the shuttering should be coated with vaseline or heavy duty grease or oil (to stop the concrete from sticking to the wood). A plywood or hardboard base should be coated with grease in the same way.

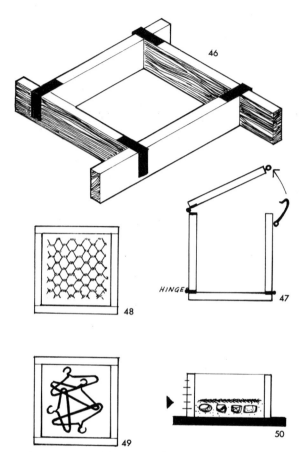

46

HINGE

47

48

49

50

To reinforce these slabs, use $\frac{1}{2}''$ or 1" chicken wire mesh (Fig. 48) or metal coat hangers (Fig. 49). Both the mesh and the coat hangers are galvanised against rust, so there should be no orange coloured stains appearing through the concrete. If you use the chicken wire, make sure you cut it 1" smaller all round than the inside of the wooden shuttering box. This will make it impossible for bits of wire to stick out from the sides of the finished slab. Lift up the chicken wire or coat hangers with bits of broken brick or stone to about $1\frac{1}{2}''$ above the baseboard (Fig. 50).

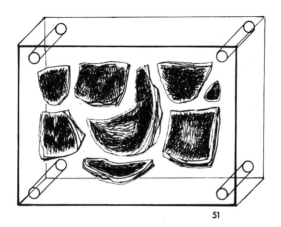

51

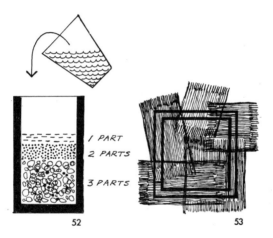

1 PART

2 PARTS

3 PARTS

52   53

Mix with water to a consistency of thick bread dough a coarse concrete aggregate made of one part portland cement, two parts sand and three parts coarse gravel (Fig. 52). Pour this aggregate three inches deep into the shuttering box. If possible, before the bottom layer sets, add 1" of top cement layer (one part portland cement, three parts fine sand). 10% hydrated lime will help to make either mix easier to work. In this way a 4" deep sandwich block will become one integral concrete slab.

If you do not intend to make large quantities of these slabs at one time, the several varieties of ready mixed mortars like Marleymix (Ace-Crete or Sacrete in U.S.A.) in one hundredweight bags are convenient and easy to use.

Large pebbles, broken ceramic tiles and dishes may be pushed into the top wet layer of these slabs.

When the slabs of concrete have set and cured, they can then be separated easily from their wooden shuttering.

It is most important that the wet concrete slabs and their mosaic surface should be allowed to dry or 'cure' slowly. In order to retard the drying, cover the concrete slab with damp newspapers or sacks (Fig. 53), remembering from time to time to remoisten this covering. The longer you can cure the concrete, the less likely you are to discover delayed cracking in the slabs. Drying should take approximately from three to seven days. When dry, you can assemble and arrange your slabs in the garden. Make sure that the ground is level, otherwise the concrete may be cracked by continuous rocking. Bed the slabs in a thin layer of sand or fine gravel about 1″ to 2″ deep; this will prevent any tendency of the slabs to rock.

You may want to cast an irregular or free form shape in concrete. My advice would be to make your concrete casting on the actual site where you want the slab to finally lie. Cut away the grass or top soil to a depth of about 4″ to 6″ and then follow the workshop casting method.

The main difference in procedure will be the need for a more flexible shuttering material (such as plywood, heavy duty lino, rubber belting etc.) that will bend into curves.

The use of Perspex or Plexiglas as a support for mosaics is a new and very dramatic way of displaying them (Fig. 51). Use only the thinnest glass smalti or stained glass tesserae and stick them with a clear epoxy resin (see chapter 6) to a ¼″ sheet of clear Perspex. Leave about a 1″ border of Perspex all round, and drill holes in the four corners to take the fixing screws.

To develop this method, suspend the Perspex support from the window, ceiling or room divider (using nylon or Terylene rope). Illuminate the panel from behind with natural or artificial light.

One important final point, take great care over measuring, and check all your measurements twice before you cut away any material.

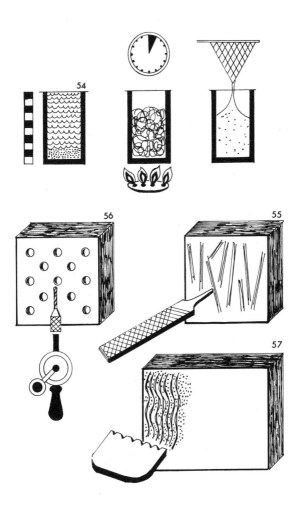

Above and right
Two tablemats designed and made by Derek Harris of Design Crafts,
who supply the frames and materials in kit form

6 Adhesives and grouts

Adhesives

In the previous chapter I have described the traditional material for attaching mosaic tesserae to a wall or slab.

Today the simplest way to fix mosaic pieces to a surface is to use the wide range of prepared adhesives that are on the market.

There are two basic types of adhesive required in the making of mosaics.

1 Temporary adhesives like flour and water paste, rubber solution and gums.

2 Permanent adhesives such as quick setting contact glues or the slower setting tile cements, or the most permanent of all, the epoxy resins like Araldite.

Temporary adhesives are used to attach the individual pieces of mosaic face down on to the full size drawing (the indirect method). When the mosaic has been turned over and is the right way up, the paper designs appear stuck to the face of the mosaic.

A good recipe for flour and water paste is one part flour to eight parts water. Stir and boil for five minutes then strain any lumps out (Fig. 54). This flour paste is easily removed together with the paper from the face of your mosaics by moistening the paper with warm water and then scraping off with a plastic scraper or scrubbing brush.

A rubber cement like Cow gum can be used in the same way as flour paste. It may be removed when dry by rolling up the gum between the fingers until you produce a ball of paper mixed with gum. Rubber solution is useful because its removal from a mosaic is an entirely dry process.

The permanent adhesives subdivide into the contact (setting immediately on contact) like Evo-Stik, UHU glue and Bostik No. 1, and the slower setting tile adhesive cements (mastic cements) like Richafix and Polybond, and Pecora rubber base emulsion in the U.S.A.

The contact adhesives are usually more expensive, and you cannot move the pieces after you have pressed the two surfaces together. They do have the advantage of being very strong (even on comparatively smooth surfaces), and are also useful in bonding two different materials together.

Another advantage is that most contact glues tend to be more transparent than the tile cements. This can be important when you want to stick tesserae in high relief without grouting.

The usual procedure when using contact adhesives is to clean and dry the surfaces to be joined. Apply a thin coat of the adhesive to both surfaces and then allow to dry for fifteen minutes. After this stage, the two adhesive films will unite immediately with only hand pressure.

For many mosaicists, the cheaper price and the slower setting time makes tile cements their choice of adhesive. There is no doubt that when you are working directly setting small pieces of tesserae, even when you have an accurate drawing to work from, it is most useful to be able to move the pieces about as you develop your design ideas. Tile cements require a baseboard surface that has been thoroughly scored (with the tang end of a file), Fig. 55, or a series of shallow holes drilled in it to lock the tile cement firmly in.

A mosaic and tile cement of this type is Fixtite; it can be used on most surfaces such as wood, hardboard, asbestos, cement etc. This is how you proceed.

1 Make sure that the surface to be covered is clean and free from grease, dust etc. There is no need for the surface to be thoroughly dry as in the case of rubber based adhesives.

2 Apply cement by means of a notched spreader to a thickness of approx 1/32 inch.

3 Now press tesserae gently into place.

4 For large areas or where you wish to make an uneven depth of cement, you may make a mix of two parts of sand to one of Fixtite.

5 Do not use this type of cement where it is liable to be continuously saturated with water.

6 Where condensation exists (bathrooms, kitchens) or on exterior work, a waterproof type of grouting should be used.

7 Any part of mosaic adjacent to the ground should also be made waterproof.

8 Tools, tesserae and hands are cleaned off with water before fixative has set.

When you are using any of the permanent adhesives mentioned, start at one corner of the base board covering a small area at a time (Fig. 57). Don't forget to use your notched spreader to even out the glue or tile cement.

The two most powerful and permanent adhesives available today are the epoxy resins and polyester resin reinforced with glass fibre (Fibreglass).

Both these are fairly expensive, although they become relatively cheaper the larger the quantity you buy at one time.

Sometime the problem may arise of how you could cantilever out at right angles from your support panel large mosaic covered forms. The weight of these shapes can cause servere leverage strains to develop, so that after a time these pieces may break and fall off.

Severe and prolonged climatic conditions of hot, cold or wet can sometimes affect the contact glues and tile cements as well as concrete. Epoxy resins and Fibreglass are unlikely to be affected by extreme conditions, but they do require much more care in preparation and application than other adhesives.

An epoxy resin is usually a two component adhesive, one of resin and one of hardener. This type of adhesive develops a strength of over a ton per square inch when fully set.

1 Prepare proportions of resin and hardener as indicated on the directions and thoroughly mix.

2 The mixture should be usable for three to five hours.

3 Make sure that the surfaces to be joined are free from any trace of grease.

4 Apply an even film of adhesive to each surface to be joined.

5 Bring both surfaces firmly together and if possible clamp by resting a heavy weight on top of the mosaic. It is a good idea to place sheets of newspaper on the surface of the mosaic before applying the weights (books or bricks). At room temperature an epoxy resin adhesive sets hard in about twelve hours. Maximum strength, water resistance and heat resistance is not reached for three days. By applying moderate heat, setting can be speeded up (place mosaic over a radiator).

Glass fibre is used to reinforce polyester resins. Fibreglass has higher strength-weight ratios than mild steel and can replace steel at only one third of the weight of it. If you apply a Fibreglass mixture to a base board of expanded metal, you can make a strong lightweight support and adhesive all in one operation. Try out some experiments on a small scale until you have the procedure controlled.

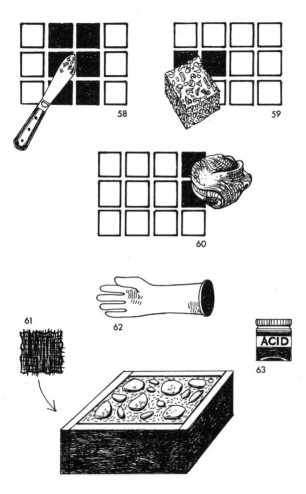

The glass fibre can be bought in kit form or you can use 'cosy wrap' type insulation blanket.
1 Inert filler powder is used as a working ingredient.
2 Pour laminating resin into a bowl and add the recommended amount of liquid hardener.
3 Tear pieces of glass fibre into a convenient size and mix them thoroughly with the resin mixture.

4 Inert filler powder should now be added and the whole mixture kneaded with the hands (use a barrier cream if you have a sensitive skin or wear rubber gloves).
5 The mixture can now be applied and squeezed into the expanded metal support.
6 It will become stickier as it is worked, so add more filler powder to counteract this.
7 Pieces of tesserae can be pushed face up into the dough-like mix.
8 The working life of the mixture is between thirty to forty minutes, so only mix and spread a small quantity at a time.

Soft plastic bowls should be used for mixing these adhesives, so that if any surplus mixture sets it can be removed by flexing the bowl. Clean and dry tins or disposable waxed paper cups are a useful alternative for mixing containers.

Grouts and grouting

After you have set the tesserae in a bed of adhesive, you will nearly always want to fill the narrow gap left between the pieces of mosaic, and level the surface of your panel. A smooth surface is very important in coffee table or garden path mosaics. This method of filling and levelling is known as grouting.

For large mosaics, mix with water one part of portland cement to three parts of sand; the sand lessens the tendency of pure cement to crack. Always remember to moisten the area to which the new cement is to be applied, otherwise you may not bond your cement grout properly. When the cement grout is dry, you can clean the face side of your tesserae with a 25% solution of hydrochloric acid (spirit of salts) Fig. 63. Remember always to wear rubber gloves. Copper or nylon kitchen scouring pads are also very useful for cleaning a mosaic after grouting; the softer copper or nylon is less likely to scratch the surface than steel wool (Fig. 61).

For mosaics that will be displayed inside the house or sheltered patio, you will need a suitable water and fungus resistant grouting cement. A standard tile grout such as Polygrout powder is mixed simply with water and allowed to stand for five to ten minutes. It stays workable for up to three hours. To apply Polygrout:

1 Press the grout well into the joints between the tesserae with a putty knife or old kitchen knife (Fig. 58).
2 Smooth off and clean off grout from face of mosaic with a damp sponge or plastic spatula (Fig. 59).
3 After the grout is dry, polish the tesserae with a coarse muslin rag or with old newspapers (Fig. 60).

Another simple method is to use Fixtite waterproof grout. This you mix to a thick creamy consistency by slowly adding water to the powder, and apply as one would for any normal grouting. Allow to dry but not harden, then clean off.

One important point about grouting is that you can colour your grey to white grouts with almost any powder water colour. Always mix the powder colour with a little water, then pour it into the cement or grouting powder.

For more permanent colour results, you can use Febtone (obtainable at most builders' merchants) or any lime-resistant dry colours. By mixing Febtone powder colours with your grout, a wide range of colour can be produced.

It is a good idea to have a selection of dry lumps of coloured grout (with the recipe attached) in your workshop. These colour samples will give you some idea of the final colour; most coloured grouts dry lighter in tone. A coloured grout that contrasts less starkly with your tesserae can help to pull together the design of your mosaic.

Coffee tables designed and made by Derek Harris

7 Projects to make

Paper mosaics

A most attractive and original way of decorating your rooms for a party or at Christmas is to make your own paper mosaics. You will also find that children are kept happy and occupied preparing paper mosaics on those long rainy afternoons in the school holidays.

Paper mosaics are good starter projects for anybody who is not sure whether he is going to enjoy making mosaics.

1 To support your mosaic, obtain some large sheets of cheap paper (coloured sugar paper, brown paper or newspaper will do). Stick the sheets together by using wide Scotch tape or gummed paper strip. If you use newspaper, this should be reinforced on back edges and across with gummed paper strip.
2 Collect all varieties of coloured paper, metal-foil from food wrappings, corrugated paper, sweet wrappers, magazines etc.
3 Draw the outlines of your design lightly in chalk.
4 Cut your coloured paper into 'tessera' squares and paste them down with any paper paste or gum.
5 For the backgrounds use larger pieces of torn paper. A good idea is to use a similar texture from the same source, i.e., silver paper wrappings, magazine fashion photographs,the pink Financial Times.
6 Stick the finished mosaic to wooden laths at the top and bottom. This stops the paper sheet curling up.
7 Attach two small screw eyes into the top lath and tie a cord.
8 Hang the paper mosaic on a wall or suspend from the ceiling like carnival flags or bunting.

Here are five useful and decorative objects which you might like to make. All the non-mosaic materials and accessories should be available at your local shopping centre.

The designs are only given as a guide. You can change or adapt them to suit your choice.

Christmas paper mosaics by Charlotte, Harriet and James Berry

51

A house name plate

1 Take a square aluminium pie or baking tin to support and frame your mosaic (Fig. 64).

2 Use a sheet of black Formica either twice the size of the pie tin (Fig. 65) for a vertical positioning, or three times larger than the tin for a horizontal positioning.

3 Place the tin on top and at one end of the Formica.

4 Cut a piece of $\frac{1}{2}''$ thick marine quality plywood the same size as the Formica and give it three coats of aluminium paint on both sides and edges.

5 Stick the Formica sheet to the plywood support with Evo-Stik.

6 Drill and screw five brass screws through the pie tin via the Formica into the wood support (Fig. 66). Use slightly over length screws. After screwing, file down the points protruding at the back.

7 Screw two heavy brass mirror brackets on to the back of the plywood panel. Take care not to screw into the Formica face side.

8 Space carefully and stick (with Evo-Stik) white plastic house name letters. Try and obtain letters that have no visible screw holes (Figs 68 and 69).

9 Use white and cream broken household tiles for the background area in the mosaic. Obtain better quality ceramic mosaic for the trunk and leaves. Best quality Byzantine smalti chippings should be used for the red and orange apples. For the trunk and leaves, use broken coloured glass mixed with ceramic tesserae (Fig. 70).

10 Stick the tesserae to the inside of the pie tin with contact adhesive. Use a white waterproof grout.

11 The completed panel can be fixed to brickwork using a masonry bit to drill the holes. Fill these with Philplug. Expanding bolts can also be used for brick or concrete. Screw or bolt the name plate to woodwork.

An original idea that can be developed from the mosaic name plate is to use a sheet of $\frac{1}{4}''$ thick clear Perspex or Plexiglas instead of the pie tin. Use coloured translucent Perspex tesserae, and stick them with Tensol No. 7 all acrylic cement, cold setting. Illuminate the mosaic from the rear at night. Do not forget to cut windows in the Formica and plywood support. The Perspex should be about $\frac{1}{2}''$ larger all round than the hole cut in the Formica and wood. This will

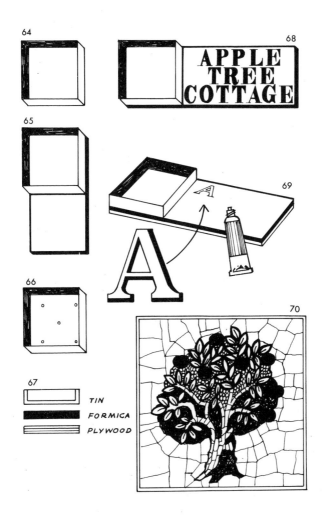

64

68

APPLE
TREE
COTTAGE

65

69

A

66

67

TIN
FORMICA
PLYWOOD

70

allow for attaching the Perspex and Formica. You can use
Evo-Stik to attach Perspex to Formica, but I should use
cadmium plated self-tapping screws as well for a really safe
job.

Mosaic coffee table

You will see that in this coffee table design I have limited the surface covered by mosaic to a comparatively small area. This design cuts down the overall weight of the table, and the mosaic disc acts as a plate on which to stand hot containers. The location and screwing of table legs is less likely to cause damage to the mosaic surface. I believe also that a contrast between two materials (with also the contrasting shapes, circle and rectangle) can sometimes be less monotonous than large areas of one material only.

It is of course also possible to buy complete kits for making mosaic tables (see list of suppliers). These usually include suggested designs, but it is much more rewarding to create your own. Some striking examples of circular tables are shown in the colour plate on p. 70.

1 Select a piece of $\frac{1}{2}''$ thick plywood (either gaboon or birch faced). The size 32" x 16" will give exactly nine table tops from a standard sheet of 8' x 4' plywood, or you may obtain suitable off-cuts from your local timber yard. An excellent coffee table top can be made from an old mahogany or oak draw table 'leaf'. Scrape the old French polish off with a steel scraper, then apply with fine steel wool two coats of clear polyurethane (Valspar) varnish.

2 Cut (with a fret or coping saw) a 12" diameter hole to one side of the table top (Fig. 71). Now brush on two coats of clear varnish, not forgetting to brush the edges of the hole.

3 With your fret or coping saw cut a plywood (or $\frac{1}{4}''$ thick hardboard) 14" diameter disc as a base board support for the mosaic area. Give both edges of the table around the hole and the disc a skim of glue, and screw the disc up to the table top (Fig. 72). The sides of the cut hole will become the frame of your mosaic.

4 Make a squared-up design full size (12" diameter circle) indicating the placing of the tesserae (Fig. 73).

5 To make the mosaic surface as flat as possible, proceed with the indirect method (Chapter 4).

6 Attach the table legs by screwing the leg top plates 2" in from the table corner (Fig. 74). If you attach the legs too far under the table, it is liable to tip over.

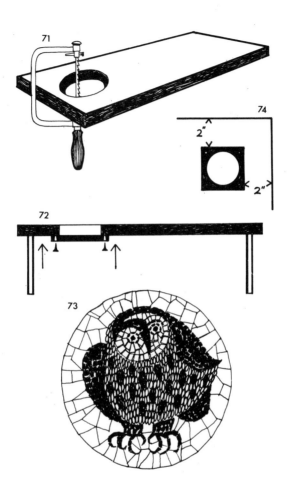

7 Apply a final coat of polyurethane clear varnish to the wooden parts of the table. When it is dry, rub down lightly along the wood grain to give a matt finish. Wax polish in the same way as any piece of wood furniture.

Mosaic door push

A mosaic door push can easily be wiped clean and resists steam and moisture. It is therefore particularly suitable for kitchens or doors leading in from the garden or patio.

1 Obtain a round or rectangular alloy pie tin about 4" to 6" in diameter or 8" x 5". This dish, similar to the one used in the first project, acts as a combined support and frame for your mosaic (Fig. 77).

2 Strengthen the pie tin by cutting a sheet of $\frac{1}{4}$" oil tempered hardboard or plywood 'washer' to fit inside the tin (Fig. 78). Before fixing the wood sheet, apply two coats of aluminium paint to the back, front and edges.

3 Cut a 1" x 1" square 'U' section aluminium channel approximately $4\frac{1}{2}$" long (Fig. 76). Use two pieces for the rectangular tin.

4 Drill the aluminium channel, the tin and the wood washer to take four $2\frac{1}{2}$" long steel screws (Fig. 79).

5 Assemble them and screw them into door stile. Make sure you do not screw into the thin door panel or into the cavity in a flush panelled door.

6 Make a squared full size design (Fig. 75) and proceed with either the direct or indirect method of mosaic application. Ceramic mosaic is the best material to use, as it will not scratch the hands when the door push is in use.

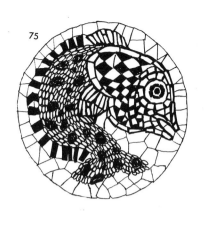

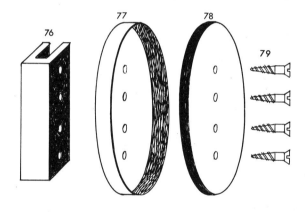

Lampbase

Most lampshades direct light downwards, and so the reflected colour and light from a mosaic covered lampbase will be shown to full avantage. You can use bottles decorated as shown on p. 61, but one of the best supports (both heavy and durable) is an unglazed drainpipe (Fig. 80) or one of the several varieties of clay cavity blocks used in building non load-bearing walls (Fig. 81).

If you wish to extend the height of your lampbase, use one block on top of the other. Always use an epoxy resin adhesive to stick them together.

1 Start by drilling a $\frac{1}{4}$" diameter hole for the electric light flex cord at the bottom of the base (Fig. 82). Use a $\frac{1}{4}$" tungsten carbide tipped masonry drill, withdrawing the drill occasionally to free the hole from dust and chips. Steady pressure must be applied, but care should be taken to avoid overheating the drill tip.

2 Cut $\frac{1}{4}$" thick plywood lids and screw and glue a $\frac{1}{4}$" plywood flange to fit tightly into the top of the lampbase. Drill a $\frac{1}{4}$" diameter hole in the centre of the lid for the flex cord (Fig. 83).

3 Take an all brass lamp-holder with a screw fit base and screw over the flex hole in the plywood lid (Fig. 84).

4 Apply the mosaic tesserae by the direct method. To stop the tesserae slipping out of place, work up from the bottom of the lampbase. Push a rolling pin over cylinder shaped bases to bed down the mosaic (Fig. 85).

5 Run the electric light flex cord through the hole in the lampbase up through the hole in the lid to the brass lampholder.

6 Cut and stick with a contact glue a hardboard or pressed cork bottom to the lampbase to avoid scratching polished furniture (Fig. 86).

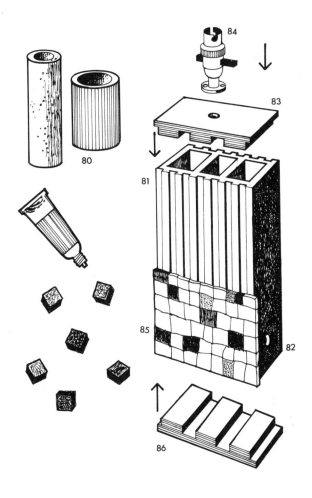

80

84

83

81

85

82

86

Bottles with mosaic decoration, suitable for lamp bases,
by part-time students at Isleworth Polytechnic

Garden or patio pebble mosaic

This is the most ambitious and also the most complicated of the projects for you to make. As a unique feature either in your front garden or in a terrace in the rear garden, you will be adding to the value and desirability of your property.

You will find it easier to cast the concrete slab for the pebble mosaic in situ (i.e. in its final position).

1 Cut turf and top soil to a depth of at least 4½". Sprinkle ½" of washed sand over the levelled pit bottom.

2 Place and fix the outer frame shuttering. The shuttering can have a thin coat of oil on the inside surface to ease separation from concrete.

3 Pour grey coloured concrete using 6lbs of black Febtone to one part of portland cement to three parts of aggregate (aggregate equals two parts sand, three parts gravel) (Fig. 87).

4 Gently press plywood letter stencils into the moist cement and leave for approximately fifteen to thirty minutes. Remove stencils (Fig. 88).

5 When the grey concrete has set, gently remove the shuttering.

6 Assemble the shuttering to form the triangular corners of the compass symbol.

7 Pour white concrete into the triangular areas, a similar mix to stage 3, but do not add colour this time (Fig. 89).

8 Place large flat stones 'edgewise' in the concrete (Fig. 90). Press all the stones into the concrete firmly, otherwise the stones may be loosened as they are walked upon. Allow to set and remove the shuttering.

9 Place the shuttering for the centre circle (a rubber dustbin lid etc.). You may have to prop the improvised circular shuttering up on bits of brick to raise the top of the shuttering up to ground level (Fig. 91).

10 Pour the same grey mix as the outer border. Push medium size dark coloured pebbles into this area and allow the concrete to set.

11 Remove the circular shuttering and finally pour a mix of white concrete (Fig. 92). Into this area place a random pattern of small coloured stones as close together as possible.

12 Cover the pebble mosaic with damp sacks and 'cure' the concrete for five to seven days.

GREY

GRASS

PIT

SAND

SHUTTERING

87

88

NO

DUSTBIN LID

91

WHITE

89

NORTH

WEST

SHUTTERING

EAST

SOUTH

90

WHITE

NORTH

WEST

EAST

SOUTH

92

13 To remove excess concrete from the surface of the pebbles, use a stiff wire brush and hydrochloric acid (spirits of salts). Wear a pair of rubber gloves to protect your hands from the acid.

8 Workplace and tools

Before I list the basic requirements for both the ideal work-shop and the acceptable compromise that most of us eventually work in, a preliminary word of advice.

The assembly of a mosaic is rarely accomplished in one go. As your projects become more ambitious, they will almost certainly require several different work periods to complete. If you leave your work in progress, do remember to make sure that it is left inaccessible to young children or pets, who may swallow or cut themselves on the mosaic materials or equipment left lying about.

The ideal workplace would be a well insulated shed or room measuring about 24' x 12' wide, lit by natural light from the sides or above. An easily washed and cleaned floor of linoleum or quarry tiles, with a large sink in one corner and some way of heating water (gas or electric ring) would also be desirable. In the middle of the work shop, or as near the main light source as possible, you should place a strongly built kitchen table or bench. If the top of this table is worn or split, resurface it with $\frac{1}{4}''$ thick oil tempered hardboard, which will make a smooth, water resistant work surface. Another refinement to your work bench would be to cover the top with either zinc or a Formica type sheet.

You cannot have too much shelf space, or cupboards with plenty of shelving inside them.

Artificial lighting can take the form of an adjustable lamp of the Anglepoise type, although I prefer the efficient overall illumination of fluorescent strip lighting.

Some form of heating in winter is essential (you cannot work with numb fingers), but this will be a choice influenced by your existing domestic system. An extraction fan fitted into the wall nearest your bench would remove the dust from your working area, but this would depend on whether the amount of time you devote to making mosaics would warrant it.

But if you live in a small house, you will probably not have any spare large rooms or sheds. You must therefore look around for a suitable compromise workspace. Perhaps the end of a garage, well lit and adequately heated, might be the answer. If you are likely to be standing for long

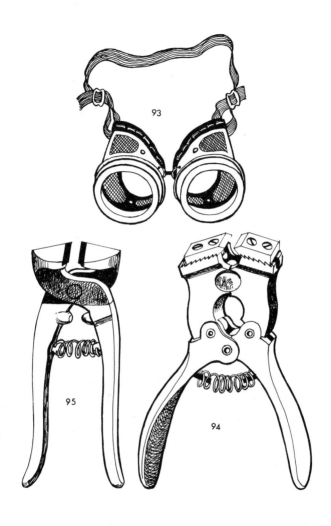

periods on a concrete floor, I would strongly recommend the use of a wooden slatted 'duckboard' or an old piece of carpet to reduce the strain on your feet.

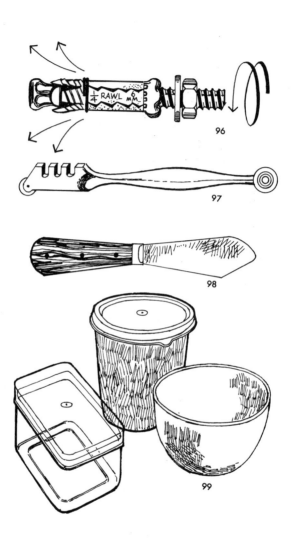

96

97

98

99

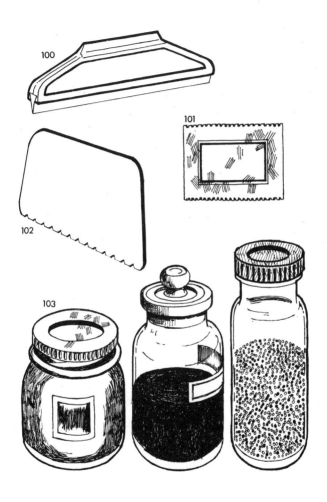

Two other suitable places for work are basements and lofts, and do not be put off if there is little or no natural lighting. Most of your early mosaic work will be done in your spare time, probably in the evening when it is dark. If the weather is warm and sunny, you can take your work outside into the garden, balcony or verandah.

Lofts can be floored with $\frac{3}{4}''$ thick chipboard, which is made in 8' x 4' panels. Assuming you can pass these sheets easily into the loft you will soon nail down a large draught proof floor. Cover the chipboard with linoleum or lino tiles for easy washing and cleaning. A sink and water supply are usually easily installed near your main roof tank.

For the flat (apartment) dweller, a deep roomy cupboard possibly built in a recess with a flap down table and carefully placed hooks and shelves - study caravan (camping) trailer storage design - can be as efficient as any much larger workshop. A cupboard workshop must be kept more tidy; therefore a sheet of heavy polythene or canvas should be placed on the floor when you are working. If none of these alternatives is available or practical, you can of course work quite comfortably on any flat surface such as the kitchen table. The main drawback of working in a living room is that you need to take extra care not to make a mess and you won't be able to leave your work in progress.

After basic space and storage requirements comes a list of the most important tools and accessories you will need. You can, of course, add or delete to suit yourself, but do not omit to buy and use the first item.

1 A safety eye shield or goggles for use when cutting or chipping mosaic materials. A lightweight pair of plastic motor cyclist's goggles is easily obtained from any motor accessory shop (Fig. 83).

2 Mosaic cutters for splitting both glass and ceramic tesserae. The adjustable head type (for cutting different thicknesses of material), Fig. 94, is the most convenient and is less tiring to use, but is also the most expensive. If you do not want to spend too much at first on tools, the simple pincer spring type cutter (Fig. 95) or tile-cutting pliers are quite adequate cutting tools.

A point to remember when choosing mosaic cutters is that the longer the handles the stronger the leverage you will be able to apply when cutting.

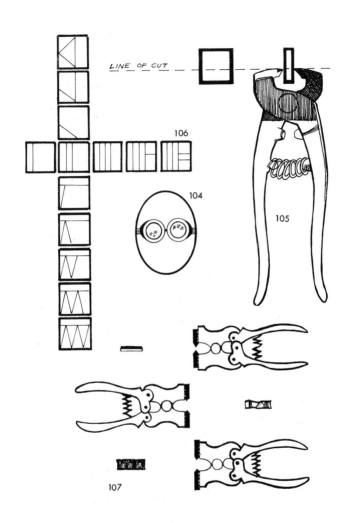

LINE OF CUT

106

104

105

107

Overleaf
Mosaic table tops made from specially glazed ceramic tiles by
Ann Wynn Reeves

3 Glass and tile cutter (Fig. 97). You should buy the simplest type. Make sure that spare cutting wheels are also available.

4 A pair of tweezers, for positioning the smaller pieces of mosaic without disturbing the adjacent tesserae.

5 A notched spreader for spreading adhesive evenly. These spreaders are often supplied with tins of adhesives (Fig. 101). If you cannot obtain a spreader, make one yourself out of hardboard or aluminium using a triangular metal file to cut the notches or teeth (Fig. 102).

6 A putty knife for applying and squeezing grout deeply and firmly in between the tesserae (Fig. 98).

7 A wooden rolling pin for pressing mosaic down into the adhesive evenly. A rolling pin is especially useful on curved surfaces.

8 A stiff but flexible plastic or rubber squeegee for scraping excess grout or adhesive from the face side of the mosaic (Fig. 100). Do not use a metal tool as this will almost certainly scratch the surface of the tesserae.

9 A wide bladed screw-driver for lifting any misplaced piece of mosaic after the adhesive has already set.

10 Brushes, cartridge paper, scissors, knife etc. for making designs and cartoons.

11 A stainless steel ruler or straight edge.

12 A small hand grindstone is a useful additional accessory for smoothing the edges of tesserae and also blobs of glaze on ceramic tesserae.

13 You will require a variety of flexible plastic (polythene) bowls and lidded buckets (Fig. 99).

14 Transparent plastic food containers make ideal tesserae storage holders that enable you to see and choose your colours easily.

15 Sheets of polythene (plastic): the horticultural grade that can be obtained from gardening suppliers by the yard up to six feet wide. Sheet polythene is useful as a semi-transparent dust sheet for covering the front of open shelving or for covering unfinished work.

16 Colour sample cards that you can make yourself from the stock ranges of tesserae. These cards mounted on hardboard and hung on the wall give you at a glance colour checks when you are working out a colour design on paper.

In addition to this list you will probably require a hammer, saw, screwdriver, drill and bits; also a square to carry out the simple carpentry required in assembling mosaic panels, tables etc. (see chapter 7).

You will need a collection of lidded containers and screw cap bottles for adhesives, grouting cements, clear varnish, turpentine and white spirit (Fig. 103).

Perhaps the tools and equipment so far mentioned appear both complicated and expensive. It is not really so, because you do not need all this equipment at once. I have included a number of items which you may like to add as your interest in mosaics develops.

Cutting mosaic

1 Always use goggles and keep your face as far away as practicable when you are cutting tesserae (Fig. 104).
2 The tesserae should be held by the thumb and forefinger. The edge of the cutters must be placed in the same line as the cut you wish to make (Fig. 105).
3 Practise cutting by dividing squares into smaller rectangles. Also, by diagonal cutting, divide a square into two triangles (Fig. 106).
4 Don't throw away wrongly cut chips of tesserae. You will always find a use for them in details etc.
5 Ceramic tile is a softer material to cut than glass mosaic.
6 Glazed ceramic tile and stained glass may be cut with standard glass cutters.
7 Mosaic cutters with adjustable jaws can be set to cut ceramic tile, smalti and thick glass (Fig. 107).

9 Making your own ceramic tesserae

When you have read this book you will probably be surprised that there are so many references to ceramic (fired clay) materials being used in all types of mosaic projects. The practical reason for this is simple. Ceramic, glazed or unglazed, is one of the most durable of man made products. In the unfired state clay is plastic (soft and easily moulded), reasonably cheap and available throughout the world.

I am not going to suggest that you should rush off and spend a lot of money setting up a fully equipped ceramic workshop. I would suggest, however, that if you cannot make your own ceramic tesserae at home, you should enquire at your local Adult Education Centre for Art and Crafts whether pottery classes are available. If these classes are well equipped with kilns etc., you should have no difficulty in making your own ceramic tesserae. But not everybody will be able to attend such classes, and even if they do, the making and firing of the ceramic materials will take much longer than in your own workshop.

The only really expensive item required is a pottery kiln (oven) to fire your clay tesserae in. The smallest suitable electric kiln, with internal dimensions 9″ cube, will cost about £35 ex. works ($ 60-100 in U.S.A.). It is also possible to find second hand kilns sometimes. It may be possible to share the price of a kiln and also subsequent firing costs with friends making pottery or mosaics themselves. A small kiln of this kind is completely safe and will plug into the ordinary domestic power plug.

The usual size for square, homemade, ceramic tesserae is about 1″ x 1″ x ¼″ to ⅜″ thick. This slightly larger size than the manufactured ceramic is to allow for a greater rate of shrinkage (you will be using clay with a greater moisture content than the manufactured variety). It also allows for cleaning and trimming the pieces when dry. Your results will probably be quite near the standard ¾″ x ¾″ pieces.

Either white, buff or red coloured clay may be used, but do not use clay sold for sculpture modelling purposes. The darker the clay, the more it will darken the glaze layer above. Many mosaicists use unglazed coloured clay for matt effects and contrasts. The clay may be coloured either by brushing over a thick, coloured, creamy mixture of clay and water, known as slip (engobe), or by colouring the clay itself. The colour is introduced into the slip by adding metal oxides. These should be added in small amounts of from 2% to 5%. Stains for colouring clay are sold by dealers in a variety of colours. These body stains are less expensive than the metal oxides and are added to clays in percentages ranging from 3% to 10%. The oxide or stain is mixed with water and poured into the slip. After stirring thoroughly, the colour-slip mixture is passed through a 60 then an 80 phosphor bronze (copper in the U.S.A.) sieve and is now ready.

To colour the clay body throughout, pour your coloured slip into a plaster mould and allow to dry until it is the consistency of bread dough.

To make a plaster mould:

1 Take a piece of clean glass and place several water colour pans upside down in the middle (Fig. 108). You can scrape a little clay on to the rim of the pans to make them stick to the glass.

2 Make a wall of clay and put it about 2″ away from the upturned pans (Fig. 109).

3 Lightly brush pans with a little soapy solution to prevent the plaster sticking to them (Fig. 110).

4 Pour dental quality plaster of Paris (obtainable from chemists) mixed with water over pans to just below the level of the clay wall. Mix 2¾lbs of plaster to each two pints of water (Fig. 111).

5 When the plaster has set, remove clay wall (Fig. 112), pans and glass and allow the mould to dry at room temperature for two or three days.

Perhaps the simplest way to make coloured clay tesserae is to dry out your slip in a plaster trough that you can make in the same way as the individual tessera mould cast from watercolour pans. Keep turning the drying slip in the plaster trough until it is the consistency of bread dough.

In order to expel all trapped air, so that it doesn't explode in the kiln during firing, it is advisable to 'wedge' the clay as follows.

1 Slap clay into an oversize brick shape (Fig. 113).

2 Place clay on strong bench or table with the nearest half slightly lifted off the bench surface (Fig. 114).

3 Slide cheese cutting wire (or nylon cord) under the clay, and pulling upwards cut the block in half (Fig. 115).

4 Lift nearest block and turn until both cut faces are towards you (Fig. 116).

5 Now slam the top block down on to the lower one (Fig. 117).

6 Turn the block half round anti-clockwise, slap it into brick-like shape and proceed to repeat process again from 1 (Fig. 118).

Continue cutting, slamming and turning at least a dozen times until there is no sign of air pockets when you cut the clay block in half.

The procedure for making self-coloured or natural clay

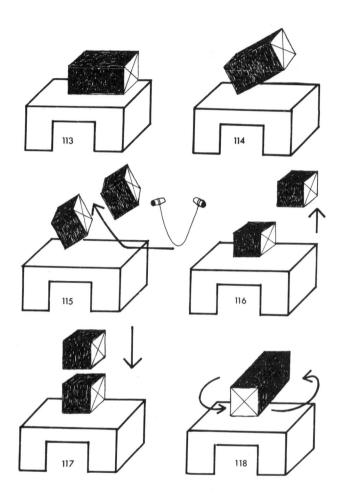

coloured standard 1″ x 1″ tesserae is the same.
1 Take a rigid flat piece of block or chipboard (about 16″ x 24″) and place it on your work table.
2 Now put a slightly damp sack or cloth over the board.
3 Place two laths about 1″ wide by ⅜″ thick along the two long sides of the board on top of the cloth.

4 Roll out with a rolling pin (similar to making pastry) a pancake of your previously wedged clay, using the laths as thickness guides (Fig. 121).
5 Make sure that your clay is the same thickness all over. Trim to a square or rectangle.
6 Mark off lightly with the tip of a knife 1" squares and cut (Fig. 119).

The square pieces of clay should be stacked for drying. To prevent warping during drying, place a piece of hardboard or a drawing board over the clay tesserae (Fig. 120). Keep turning each piece (twice a day), making sure the outer areas do not dry first. When dry, scrape any cutting ridges off with a knife and smooth down with No. 150 grade sandpaper.

Biscuit firing

Do not forget that clay must be absolutely dry right through before firing, otherwise it will explode during firing in the kiln. It is not always easy to tell when a coloured clay is dry. One way is to hold a clay piece against your cheek. If there is the slightest sensation of coldness on your cheek, the clay is almost sure to have too high a moisture content and must continue to dry out. If you make a very thick clay, shape in relief. It is a good idea to hollow out, from the under side, the thickest areas of clay. The best tool to use is a looped modelling tool.

Most simple electric kilns have a three heat switch; i.e., low, medium and high. When you are making your first or 'biscuit' firing of the clay, unless otherwise instructed, you should allow at least one hour firing on low then one hour on medium before switching on to top heat. The firing should take at least eight hours, both for biscuit and glost (glaze) firing.

A new kiln, before the elements have fully oxidised, may fire too rapidly for the first few firings. In this case you should either open the spyhole stopper slightly or keep the kiln switched on medium a little longer. Clayware may touch each other during biscuit firing. The spyhole stopper may be left out for half the firing period to allow any steam to escape from the clay. The usual temperature for firing biscuit is 1000° Centigrade. You can check this by using either Seger cones or a pyrometer temperature indicator.

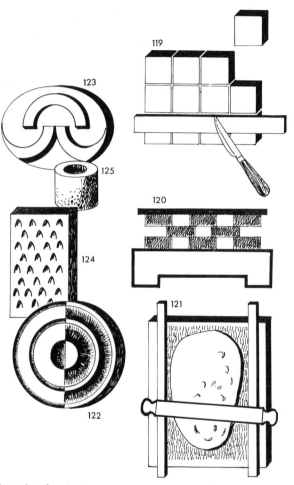

After the fired clay pieces have cooled, you can either leave them matt in texture and use them for mosaic at once, or you can cover them with a thin layer of glaze (glass).

Colour can be applied underneath a clear glaze (underglaze colour) or the glaze itself can be coloured.

You can apply underglaze colour (obtainable from pottery suppliers) mixed with water and brushed on to the biscuit clay body. A better way is to spray the colour on, using a fixitive type spray tube or any fine spray applicator. You can spray two contrasting colours to achieve speckled effects.

The glaze itself is also better sprayed on to small pieces rather than dipping them, partly because you will not have to clean off the base of the fired clay piece and partly because you are more likely to get an even layer of glaze. Coloured glaze may be opaque (with the addition of tin oxide) or clear with colour added. Both types of glaze can be obtained from your pottery supplier, or you can make them up yourself.

Glaze should be mixed with water and brushed through a 100 and then through a 20 mesh sieve. After sieving, the glaze should weigh 30 ozs to the pint. It should be stirred thoroughly before and during use. The biscuit fired clay should be free from grease and dust, otherwise the glaze may crawl. Crazing or fine cracks in the glaze are due either to underfiring or to too thick a layer of glaze.

Glaze firing

Glaze should be rubbed off the bottom of biscuited pieces before placing in the kiln. If you are using kiln shelves, three supporting props are more rigid than four. Try not to put glaze shelves opposite element slots. The glazed pieces should not touch each other or they will stick together when the glaze melts. Most coloured glazes fire aroung 1080° Centigrade, but the bright reds and oranges may fire as low as 850° Centigrade. If you are in doubt about firing temperatures, follow the manufacturer's recommendations.

The maturing of clay bodies and glazes is not so critical in making ceramic mosaic tesserae as it is in making tableware.

I believe that the main reason for making your own ceramic mosaic tesserae should be that it allows you to develop and control a greater variety of shape and size.

The basic methods that I have just described apply equally well to making circular clay discs or medallions (Figs 122 and 123), textured patterns with modelling tools (Fig. 124), low relief ceramic tiles, clay rings (Fig. 125), tubes etc.

10 Mosaics, a short historical survey

I am sure that anyone, however involved he may be in the practical application of mosaic, will want to know something about the development and history of his chosen art and craft. If you wish to read about the history of mosaic in more detail, I suggest you make a list of the main periods and styles mentioned and take it to your local public library. You should be able to find a selection of books in both the art and history sections that will tell you much more about the subject than I can possibly hope to do here.

Probably the earliest use of mosaic (4,000 to 5,000 B.C.) is to be found in the area between the rivers Tigris and Euphrates (Mesopotamia) in the Middle East. Here cones of baked clay painted red or black or just left uncoloured were pushed into a wall mortar of mud and chopped straw, leaving the flat coloured base exposed. The first designs were simple geometric patterns; later, animal and plant symbols were introduced.

From about 3,000 B.C., the Chaldean and Babylonian civilizations inlaid their domestic and ritual objects and even musical instruments such as harps with mosaic. In the British Museum you can see the Standard of Ur, which shows men and animals in battle. The tesserae are mostly minute pieces of lapis lazuli and mother of pearl.

At about the same time the Early Egyptians inlaid ivory boxes with bits of coloured glass, lapis lazuli and other stones. Sometime later, about 2,000 B.C., the Minoans in Crete used large stones and pebbles in different patterns and colours in their pavements.

The Romans (800 B.C. onwards) were the first of the early civilizations to develop and use a mosaic technique on a large scale in their towns and cities. Roman mosaic was applied to roads, city squares, and walls. Black, white, red and green marble was used to surface baths and fountains, and tesserae of glass and gold were reserved for the more sumptuous wall decorations.

The golden age of mosaic was reached during the early Christian period in Southern Italy, and in the historically parallel Byzantine period in Asia Minor.

In 326 A.D. the first Christian Roman Emperor, Constantine, commenced the building of a new city, Nova Roma, on

Detail from the mosaic in the Basilica San Vitale at Ravenna, Italy

Jeanne Reynal: **Mosaics on Two Surfaces**

the site of the ancient Greek city of Byzantium, which was later to be known as Constantinople. From 326 to 1453 Byzantine art flourished, and the most magnificent art form of the Byzantines was their mosaics. Just as it is true that Byzantine architecture cannot be considered apart from the light and colour effects introduced by the mosaics, so it is true that mosaics must be considered closely linked with the church architecture of the period.

In St Apollinare Nuova at Ravenna, Italy (early sixth century), the mosaic showing the procession of martyrs emphasises the axis of the church and introduces a rhythmical movement towards the altar. In the Baptistry of the Orthodox, which is a round building, there is a procession of apostles in the dome which makes the dome appear to rotate. The mosaics are not limited to panels, but cover the entire interiors. The result is to make the walls lose their character as limiting agents, thus creating an extensive new spiritual world.

The mosaics of San Vitale, also in Ravenna (540 A.D. to 550 A.D.), are especially famous for the representation of the Emperor Justinian and the Empress Theodora, each attended by their court followers. Although the heads of these figures have the qualities of portraits, there is little suggestion of conventional modelling. The emphasis is placed upon the pattern of the gorgeous costumes. In this single church, organised into a unified system of decoration, there is the most varied subject matter representing church history, a cycle devoted to early sacrifice, and the glorification of the Lamb and the majesty of the court.

In an early example of Byzantine art, the tomb of Galla Placida at Ravenna, the representation of the Good Shepherd, though still very close to Greek and Roman traditions, already shows a move towards the transformation from classical naturalism towards the more hieratic Byzantine expression. Above all, in Byzantine and early Christian mosaics, there is a curious mixture of mysticism and realism.

After the Justinian period, mosaic art declined. The lower walls of St Apollinare are weak imitations of the earlier period.

Technically the Byzantine mosaics developed the use of coloured glass and gold mosaic, very similar to the Byzantine smalti obtainable today. Compared to the marble of the

Romans, the glass tesserae have an almost infinite colour range and reflective qualities.

The method of applying the mosaic to church interiors was as follows. First, the surface of the vault or arch was roughened and covered with a layer of cement. On this first

Antoni Gaudi: Guell Park, Barcelona, 1900

screed a second layer of cement was added. Each piece of tessera was then individually applied by hand, using the direct method. Because the cement was still wet, it squeezed up in between the stones forming its own grouting. The grout was sometimes coloured to blend with the overall effect of the mosaic. Small cubes of mosaic were used for faces, hands and details, the larger pieces were used in the background. The brighter colours were left slightly raised from the surface; the darker colours were, in contrast, set as deeply as possible.

With the arrival of the Italian Renaissance in the 14th century and a little later the capture of Constantinople by the Turks in 1453, the art of mosaic in Europe declined into the mere imitation of painting. Inevitably the formality established by Byzantine mosaics in colour and design, that was ideally suited to the spiritual needs of the early Christian Church, was superceded by the newly rediscovered realism and humanism of the Renaissance.

The isolated civilizations of Central and South America, Inca, Maya, Aztec etc., all developed a mosaic or inlay technique, particularly in jewellery and personal adornments. Ear plugs of shell mosaic, hand shaped pendants of shell inlaid with turquoise and gold are typical mosaic pieces. The adhesive, a primitive gum or sometimes pitch, was used to stick the minute pieces of shell or semi-precious stones to the support. Other materials were garnet, gold, obsidian, malachite etc. The designs were very intricate, showing both geometric symbols and stylised beasts, men and gods. The effect of these extremely rich, almost writhing, designs was one of all over pattern, probably influenced by the highly developed textile arts in the civilizations.

In Europe towards the end of the 19th century, a young Spanish architect, Antoni Gaudi (1852-1926), working in Barcelona, began to use ceramic and glass mosaic in his buildings in a wholly new and original way.

In order to arrive at his own means of expression and in defiance and reaction against the colourless buildings of his time, Gaudi used pieces of polychrome glass and ceramic as an integrated surface feature. This almost collage-like use of mosaic was closely linked to Gaudi's curving and membranous walls and roofs that were in themselves structural inovations of great originality. In the Guell Park (1900-

Simon Rodia: Watts Towers, California

Antoni Gaudi: Guell Park, Barcelona, 1900

1914), in Barcelona, Gaudi used vast quantities of broken plates, china dolls and bottles, as well as glass and ceramic tiles (see p. 85). Apart from the almost surrealist effect of his use of mosaic materials, there is also a quality of passion and frenzy not usually found in modern church or domestic architecture.

The best place to study the more recent use of large scale architectural mosaics is in South and Central America, particularly in Mexico.

There artists have used large local stones of different colours for their outside mosaics. This method not only gives added effect to the dramatic subjects and styles used by the Mexicans, but also contributes to a monumental all over texture ideally suited to the bright sunlit climate. One of the best known examples of mural mosaic in Mexico is the University Library, Mexico City, 1952. The entire wall area of this large block is covered in prefabricated sections of mosaic designed by the painter-architect Juan O'Gorman. In 1965 O'Gorman also designed his own house as a fantastic surrealist dream creation surfaced with coloured stones. The tops of the walls are crenellated with a variety of symbols and native figures.

Another Mexican painter, Diego Rivera, designed a series of bizarre mosaics for the water works at Lerma, Mexico City, 1952. In the middle of the pool, lying half submerged, is a frightening mosaic monster made of concrete covered with natural coloured stone.

Some of the motorways in Mexico have central islands dividing the two directions of traffic. Reminiscent of Gaudi, these islands have sinuous, free form walls and clusters of isolated domes all covered with a mosaic of natural stone.

Today mosaics in the widest sense are stimulating artists, both professional and amateur, to explore the visual possibilities in all varieties of material, for colour, texture, form etc. I should now like to make an inevitably incomplete list of some of the more experimental artists using mosaic methods in a fresh and exciting way.

Lee Krasner and Ronal Stein, U.S.A. Designed 1100 sq. ft mosaic mural for office building at Number Two Broadway, New York, 1958. These artists smashed 15″ diameter sheets of Italian glass smalti (smalti are usually cut from these sheets into stones of $\frac{3}{8}″ \times \frac{1}{2}″$) into large irregular fragments for their mosaic mural. The colours used were eight earth greens, six ultramarines, four Alizarin crimsons and three blacks. Dark coloured cement grout was used throughout.

Glen Michaels, U.S.A. Uses mainly 'found objects' for his mosaics, e.g., metal stampings, keys, watch springs, broken glass, bones, weathered plywood.

David Partridge, Great Britain. Makes panel and ceiling mosaics from nails of all sizes, also painted accents of bright colour. (See p. 90.)

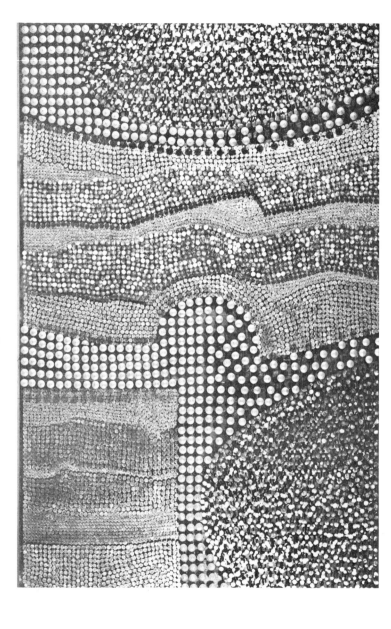

Simon Rodia: Watts Towers, California

Julio Le Parc, France. Ceiling constructions of slightly curved aluminized plastic, suspended by nylon threads. Another construction has hundreds of grey blue plastic squares, suspended by nylon threads, continuously turning and reflecting the light.
Jeanne Reynal, working in U.S.A. Apart from wall mosaics, she has made free standing constructions covered with mosaic on both sides. The shapes are mainly geometric in origin, and the materials used are glass smalti, mother of pearl, and drifts made from smalti dust. (See pp. 82-3.)

David Patridge: Nail mosaic: **Equinox,** 1965

Nicholas Vergette: Wood and ceramic panel

Above
Omero Fromboluti: Detail of bathroom mosaic

Fernand Leger, France. The late Fernand Leger designed mosaics for University City, Caracas, Venezuela, and also the American War memorial at Bastogne, Belgium.

Lewis Krevolin and Elizabeth Constantine, U.S.A. They make coffee table tops from smashed ceramic mosaic. After arranging the broken pieces, they paste newspaper over the face side and let it set. A board (the size of the table top) is clamped over the paper and mosaic pieces and turned over. Next, coloured cement is poured over the reverse side of the ceramic fragments, then the wood support is placed on the cement mosaic 'sandwich' from above. When the cement has set, the mosaic is turned right side up and the paper and first board removed. In this way the flattest table surface possible is achieved. When finished, the wooden parts of the table are given several coats of pure linseed oil.

Nicholas Vergette, British, now working in U.S.A. Has designed and constructed 400 sq. ft of mosaic walls for the Baptistry of the Cathedral of the Immaculate Conception in Syracuse, New York. The mosaic is made up of 40,000 different ceramic pieces. He uses glazed and unglazed ceramic as the dominant material (very often in relief), with backgrounds of planed end-on wood etc. (See pp. 92-3.)

Finally, I should like to mention three artists who have produced wonderful mosaic creations either in retirement or as an intensive spare time activity.

Simon Rodia for 33 years worked on three steel and concrete towers 104, 100 and 80 feet high, now known as Watts Towers, on the outskirts of Los Angeles, U.S.A. He encrusted the wet cement with thousands of bits of broken dishes, bottles and other people's rubbish to produce something like a fairyland castle. The cement was also impressed with patterns made with sea shells, kitchen utensils, tools, machinery etc. (See pp. 87 and 91.)

Fernand Cheval also spent about 30 years making his dream palace. This French postman collected coloured stones in his post bag, as he made his mail deliveries, to decorate his fantastic building.

Omero Fromboluti, Italian immigrant to U.S.A. Stonemason and cement finisher, he started to make mosaics in retirement from 1957. He uses coloured ceramic tesserae, clear and coloured glass, buttons, toy watch faces, pieces of Woolworth jewellery etc. His subjects are scenes of Italy,

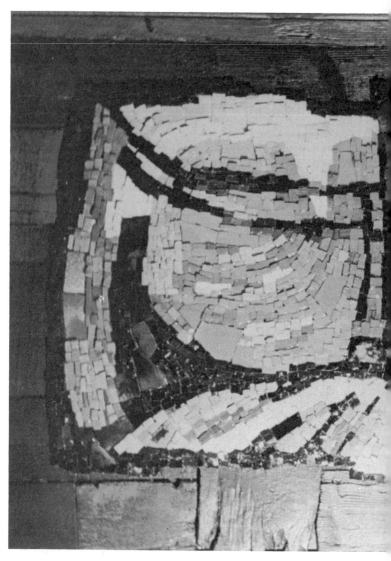

Hans Unger and Eberhard Schulze: wall panel

T.V. and film personalities, and decorative abstract patterns. Omero Fromboluti uses only one pair of cutting pliers to slit his mosaic materials. He builds a shallow box frame of heavy plywood, then places reinforcement of wire coat hangers on to the heads of large tacks already driven into the support panel. A slow drying (sometimes coloured) adhesive is then poured into the combined frame and support. Into this adhesive the artist selects and pushes his various types of materials. When set, the mosaic is complete and does not require any further attention. (See p. 94.)

For further reading

Practical Mosaics by Hans Unger. Studio Vista, London. Viking, New York.

Education of Vision edited by Gyorgy Kepes. Studio Vista, London. George Braziller, New York.

Simple Pottery by Kenneth Drake. Studio Vista, London. Watson-Guptill, New York.

Antoni Gaudi by James Johnson Sweeney and Josep Lluis Sert. Architectural Press, London. Frederick A. Praeger, New York.

How to Make Collages by John Lynch. Thames & Hudson, London. The Viking Press, New York.

Mosaics of Jeanne Reynal by Jeanne Reynal. Edited by Dore Ashon and others. George Wittenborn, New York.

Colour: Order & Harmony by Paul Renner. Studio Vista, London.

Modern Mosaic Techniques by Jenice Lovoos and Felice Peremore. Watson Guptill, New York.

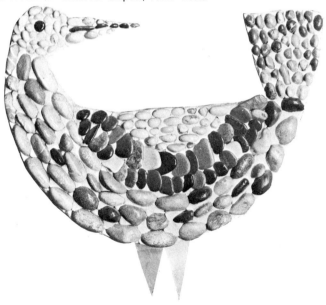

Pebble and shell mosaics by part-time students at Isleworth Polytechnic

List of suppliers

Design Crafts, 21 Crown Street, Brentwood, Essex.	Italian glass smalti Byzantine smalti Mosaic cutters and tools Mosaic kits
Edgar Udny & Co. Ltd, The Mosaic Centre, 83 & 85 Bondway, Vauxhall, London, S.W.8.	Venetian glass mosaic (gold and silver) Ceramic mosaic All mosaic tools Febstone cement pigment Fixtite tile cement
Jason Mosaics Ltd, 77a Ilderton Road, London, S.E.16.	Ceramic mosaic (Vitrified frost proof porcelain)
Cope & Co. Ltd, 8 Gray's Inn Road, W.C.1.	Richafix tile cement
Joseph Freeman & Sons Ltd, 96, Garratt Lane, London, S.W.18.	Cementone (cement pigment)
Shell Chemicals Ltd, Villiers House, 41-7, Strand, London, W.C.2.	Epikote 828 (epoxy resin)
W. David and Sons Ltd, 47-49 Caledonian Rd, London, N.1.	Isopon fibre glass kits
C.I.B.A. Ltd, Duxford, Cambridge.	Araldite (epoxy resin adhesive)

Brianco (London) Ltd,
16, Norton Folgate,
Bishopsgate, London, E.1.

Coffee table frames, legs and tops

Bullanco Ltd,
66, Queens Road,
London, S.E.15.

Aluminium sheet section, screws and self tapping screws

Britisch Ceramic Service Co. Ltd,
Bricesco House,
1, Park Avenue,
Wolstanton, Newcastle, Staffs.

Ceramic kilns and equipment

B. Webber Ltd,
Webcot Works,
Alfred Street,
Fenton, Stoke-on-Trent,
Staffordshire.

Small ceramic kilns and ceramic equipment

Glazed & Floor tile
Association,
Federation House,
Stoke-on-Trent,
Staffs.

For all information on tile and ceramic mosaic manufacturers

Imperial Chemical Industries Ltd,
Plastics Division,
Welwyn Garden City,
Herts.

Pamphlets and information about Perspex

G. H. Bloore Ltd,
480, Honeypot Lane,
Stanmore,
Middlesex.

Perspex
Plexiglas
Tensol
Oroglas

US Suppliers

Pezandie and Sperrie,
103 Lafayette,
New York, New York.

Dyes and pigments

Reynold Vedovato Corp.,
323 East 102 Street,
New York, New York.

Mastic adhesives

Drakenfield and Co.,
45 Park Place,
New York, New York.

Ceramic kiln and materials

Leo Popper & Sons,
143 Franklin Street,
New York, New York.
(Importers and Retailers)

Italian glass smalti mosaic
suppliers

Schwartz Chemical Company Inc.,
50-01 2nd Street,
Long Island City, New York.

Epoxy resins

Jack D. Wolfe Co.,
724 Meeker Avenue
Brooklyn, New York.

Ceramic clays, kilns, materials

Almost every area has a local marble dealer, tile cutter, or dealer of commercial tiles. Consult the classified telephone directory.

Index

Acknowledgements

The author and publishers would like to make the following acknowledgements for pictures in this book:

David Partridge mosaic photographs by Maurice Broomfield
Isleworth Polytechnic part-time students' work photograph by David Dunk
Simon Rodia mosaic photographs by Colin Cannon
Jeanne Reynal mosaic photograph by Peter Moore
Paper Mosaic photograph by Ted Sebley
Antoni Gaudi mosaic photograph by The Spanish National Tourist Office
Mosaics by Simon Clark and Ann Wynn Reeves photographed by Kenneth Clark